# Table of Contents

# Can You Find These Words?

art

family

protests

sports

# I See Community

I see community in friendship.

art

I see community in public **art**.

sports

# I see community in **sports**.

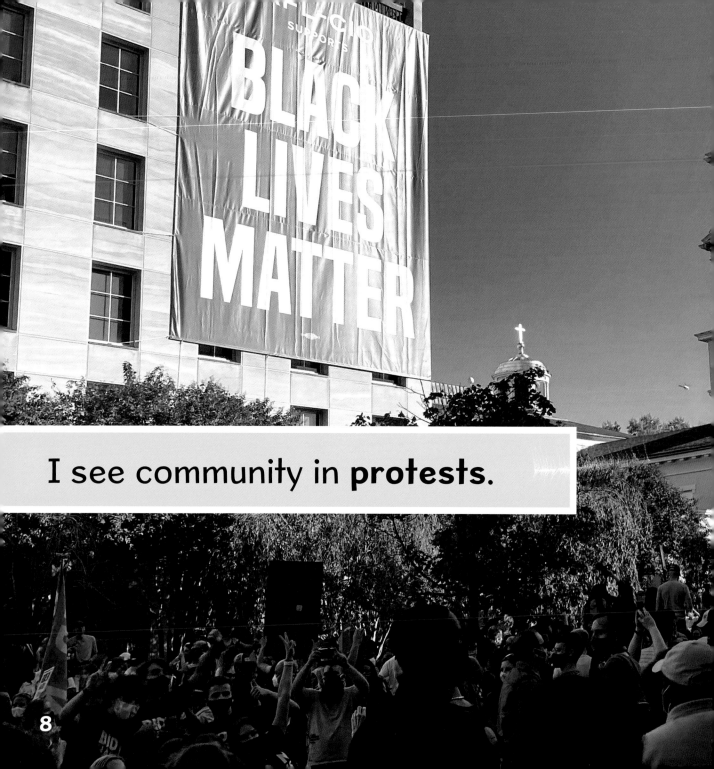

I see community in **protests.**

protests

I see community in **family.**

family

I see community in traditions.

# Photo Glossary

 **art** (ahrt): Beautiful things that are created for others to enjoy.

 **family** (FAM-uh-lee): A group of people related to one another.

 **protests** (PROH-testz): Demonstrations against something.

 **sports** (sportz): Games involving physical effort and skill.

# About the Authors/Photographers

Martin Wong is a writer from Los Angeles. When he and his family aren't spending time in Chinatown, they like to attend concerts, watch movies, check out books from the library, make art, and go on road trips.

Alma Patricia Ramirez is a writer who enjoys writing in English and Spanish for children and adults. She enjoys community activities like festivals, celebrations, and organized sports.

Allen R. Wells is a writer and mechanical engineer in Atlanta, GA. He loves having the chance to meet up with friends and family.

Kaitlyn Duling is a writer and editor. She enjoys volunteering and making friends in her Washington, DC community.

www.rourkeeducationalmedia.com

PHOTO CREDITS: cover: (background) ©Getty Images; cover, page 2, 4, 5, 12, 13, 14, 15: Martin Wong; page 2, 6, 7, 14, 15: Alma Patricia Ramirez; page 2, 3, 10, 11, 14, 15: Allen R. Wells; page 2, 8, 9, 14, 15: Kaitlyn Duling

Edited by: Hailey Scragg
Cover and interior design by: Lynne Schwaner

**Library of Congress PCN Data**
I See Community/Martin Wong, Allen R. Wells, Kaitlyn Duling, Alma Patricia Ramirez
(Life Through My Lens)
ISBN 978-1-73165-188-4 (hard cover)(alk. paper)
ISBN 978-1-73165-233-1 (soft cover)
ISBN 978-1-73165-203-4 (E-book)
ISBN 978-1-73165-218-8 (e-Pub)

Library of Congress Control Number: 2021944586

Printed in the United States of America
01-3402111937